Dragon

Coloring Book for Adults

Midnight Edition

CREATIVE COLORING PRESS

First edition: 2017

Photo credits: Shutterstock

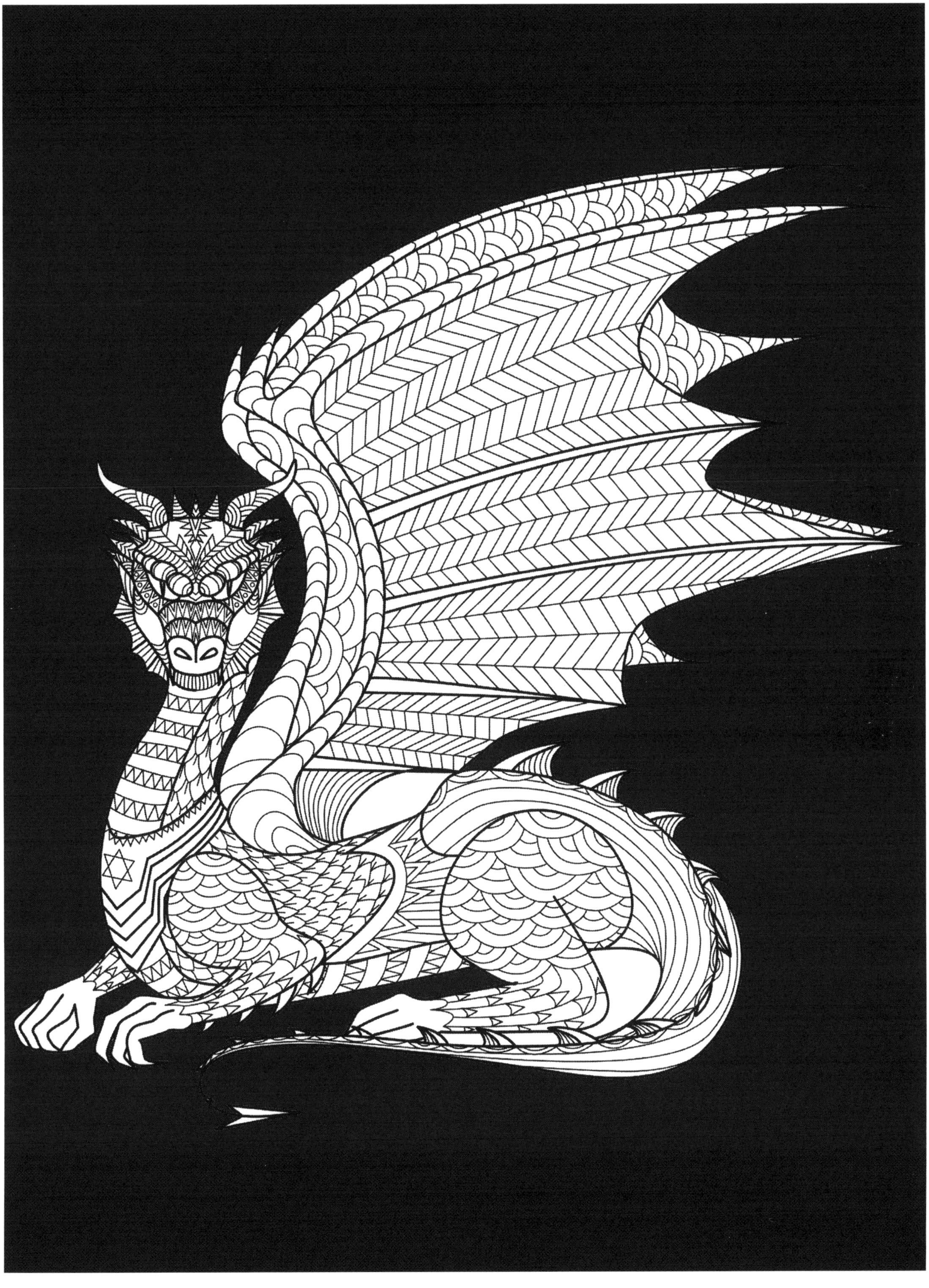

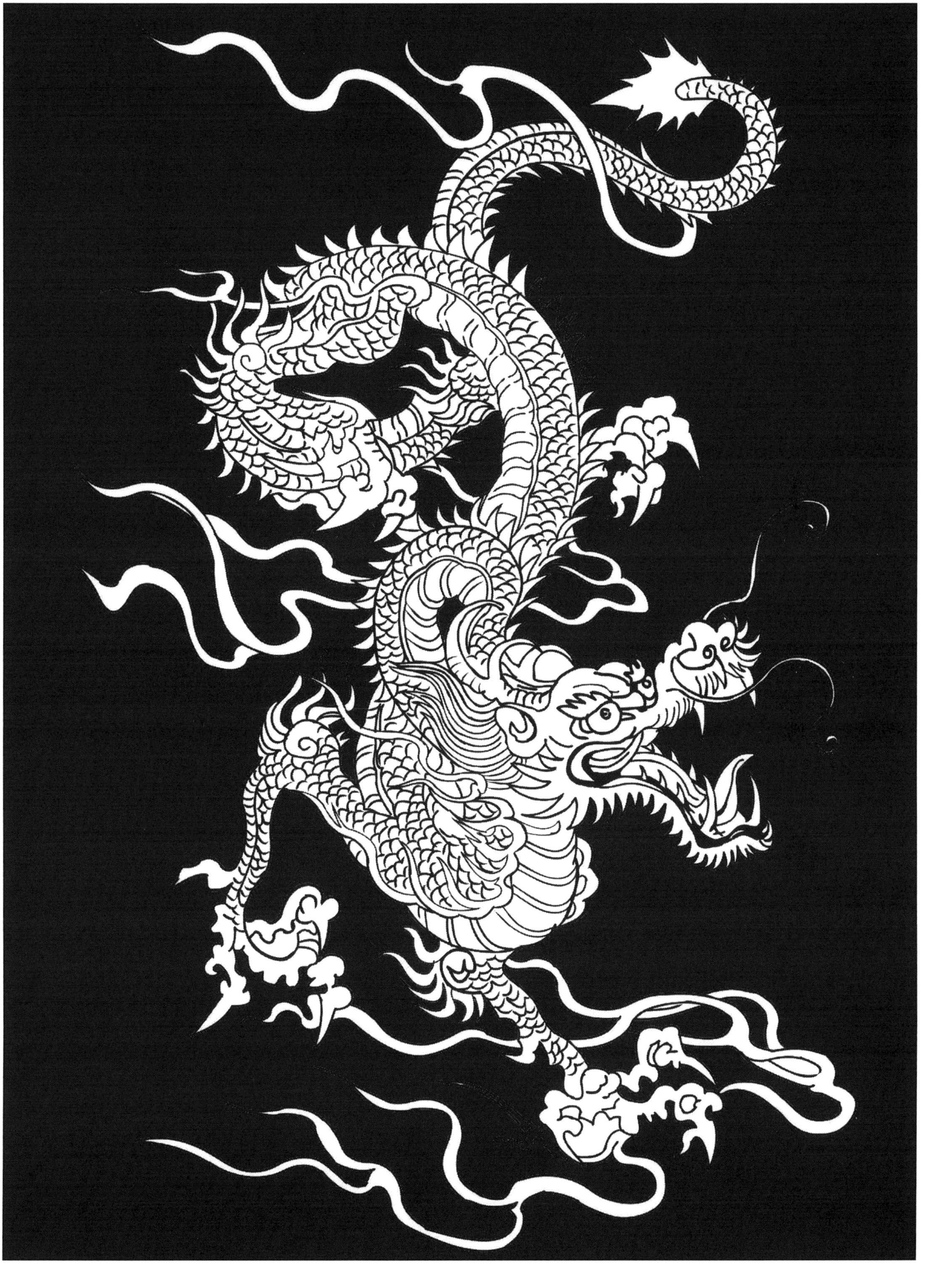

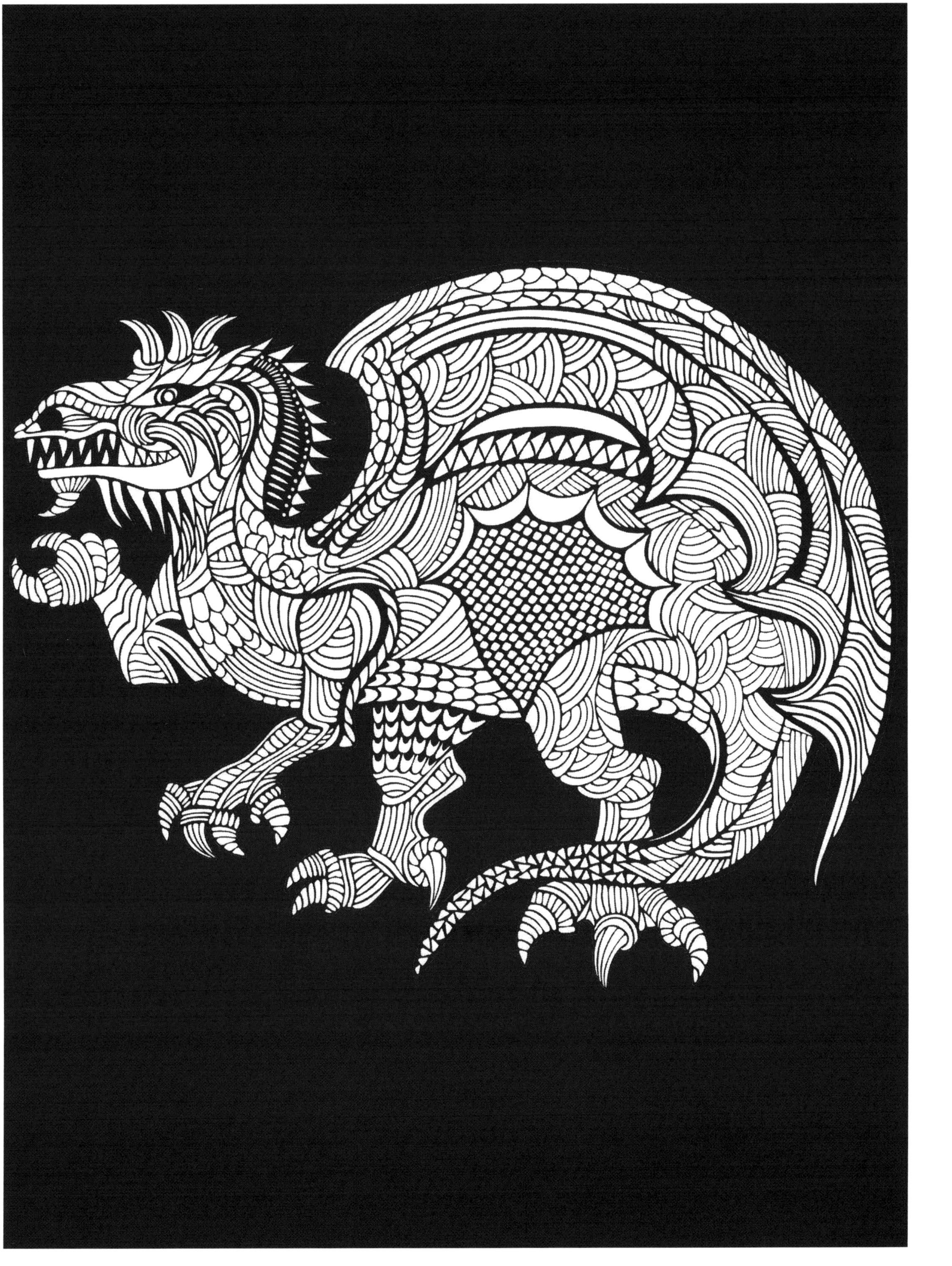

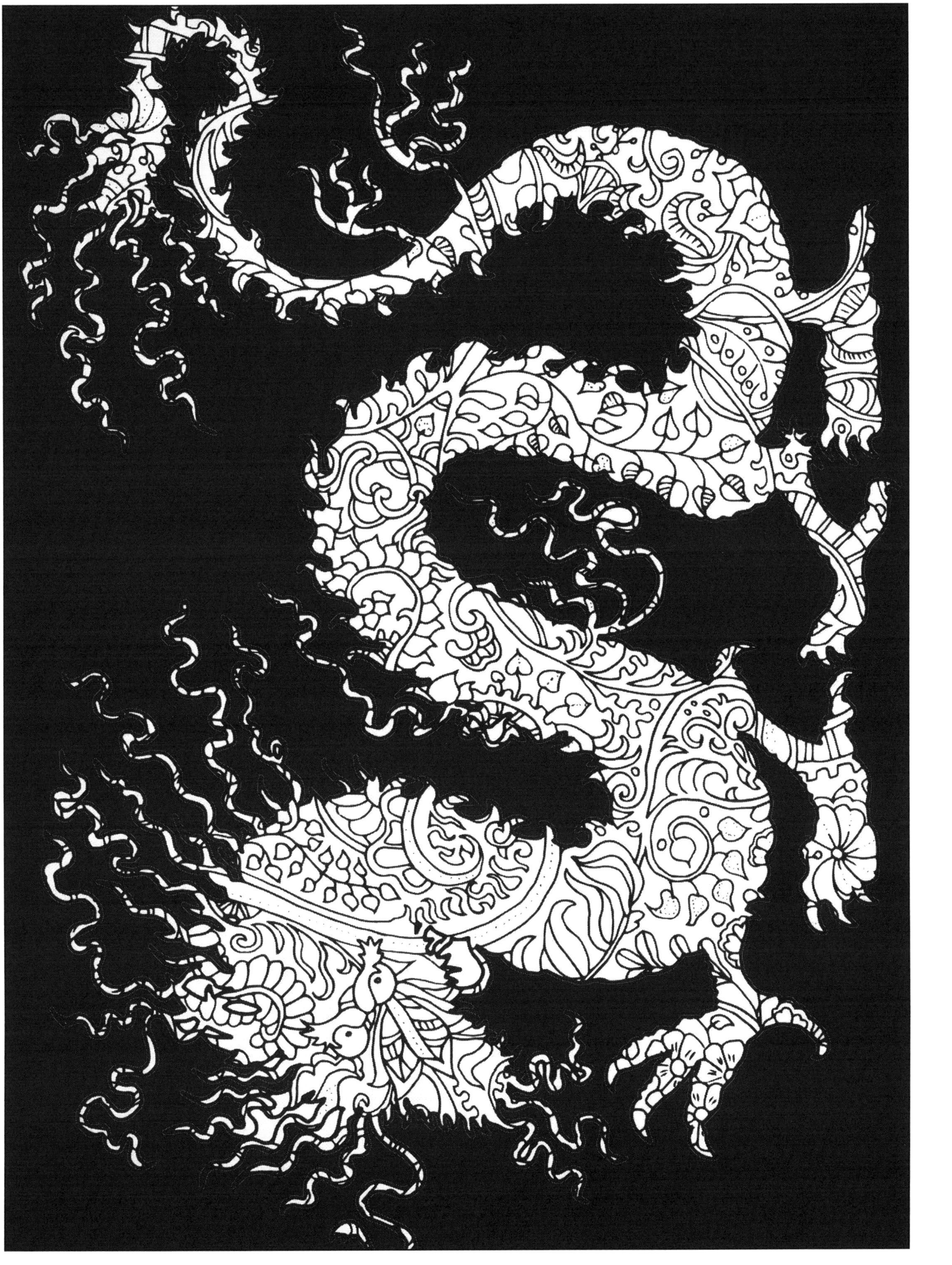

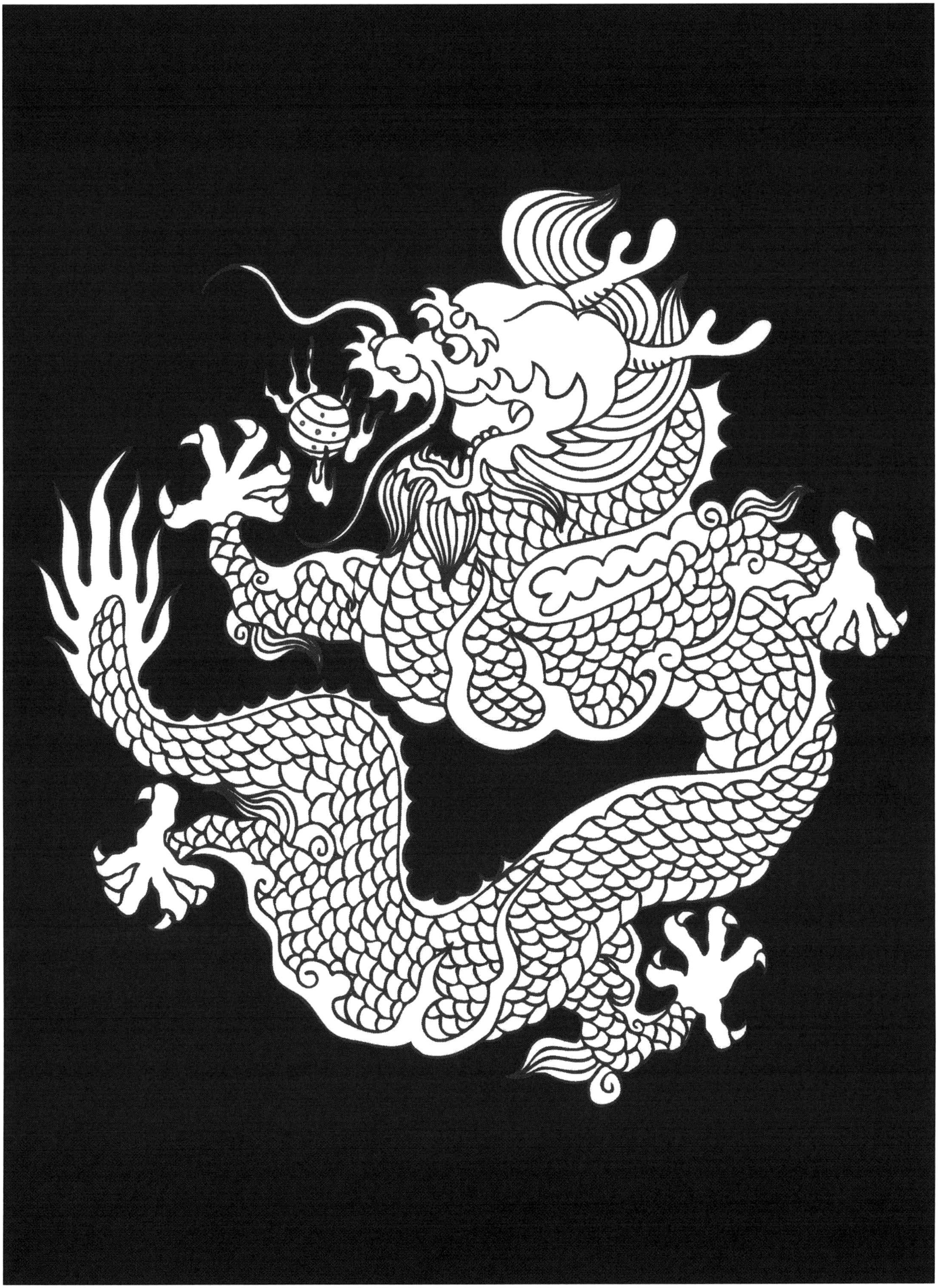

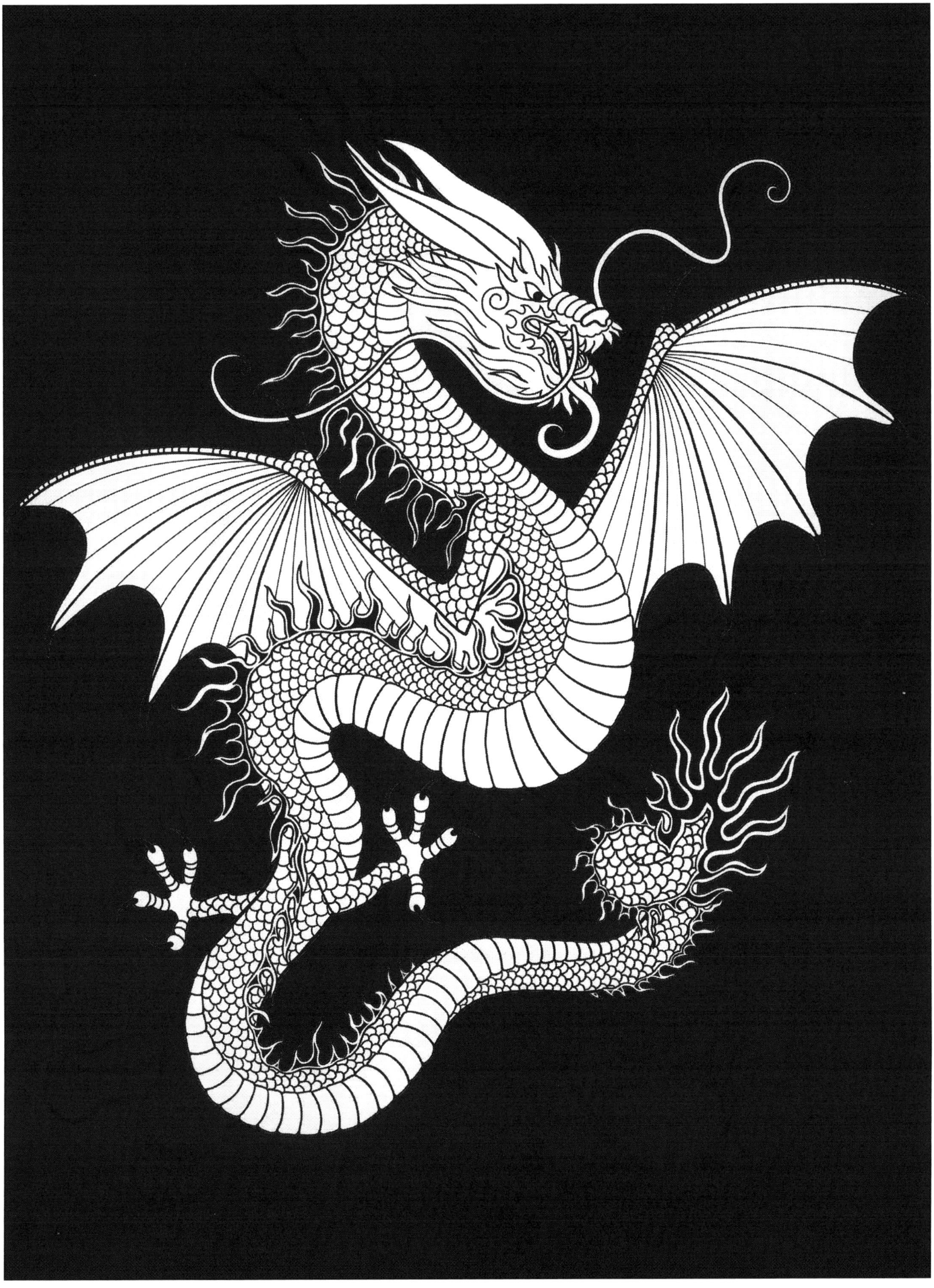

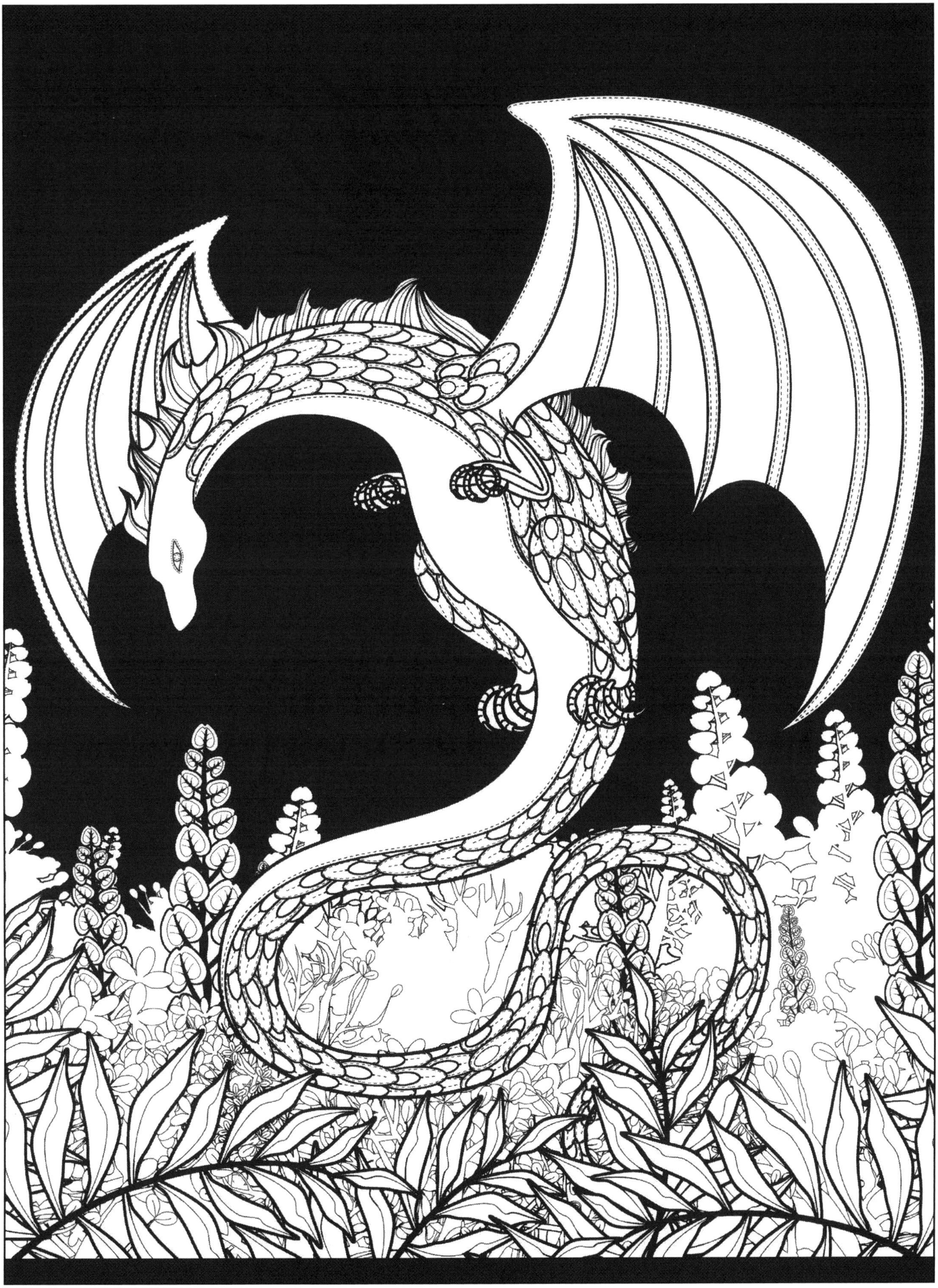

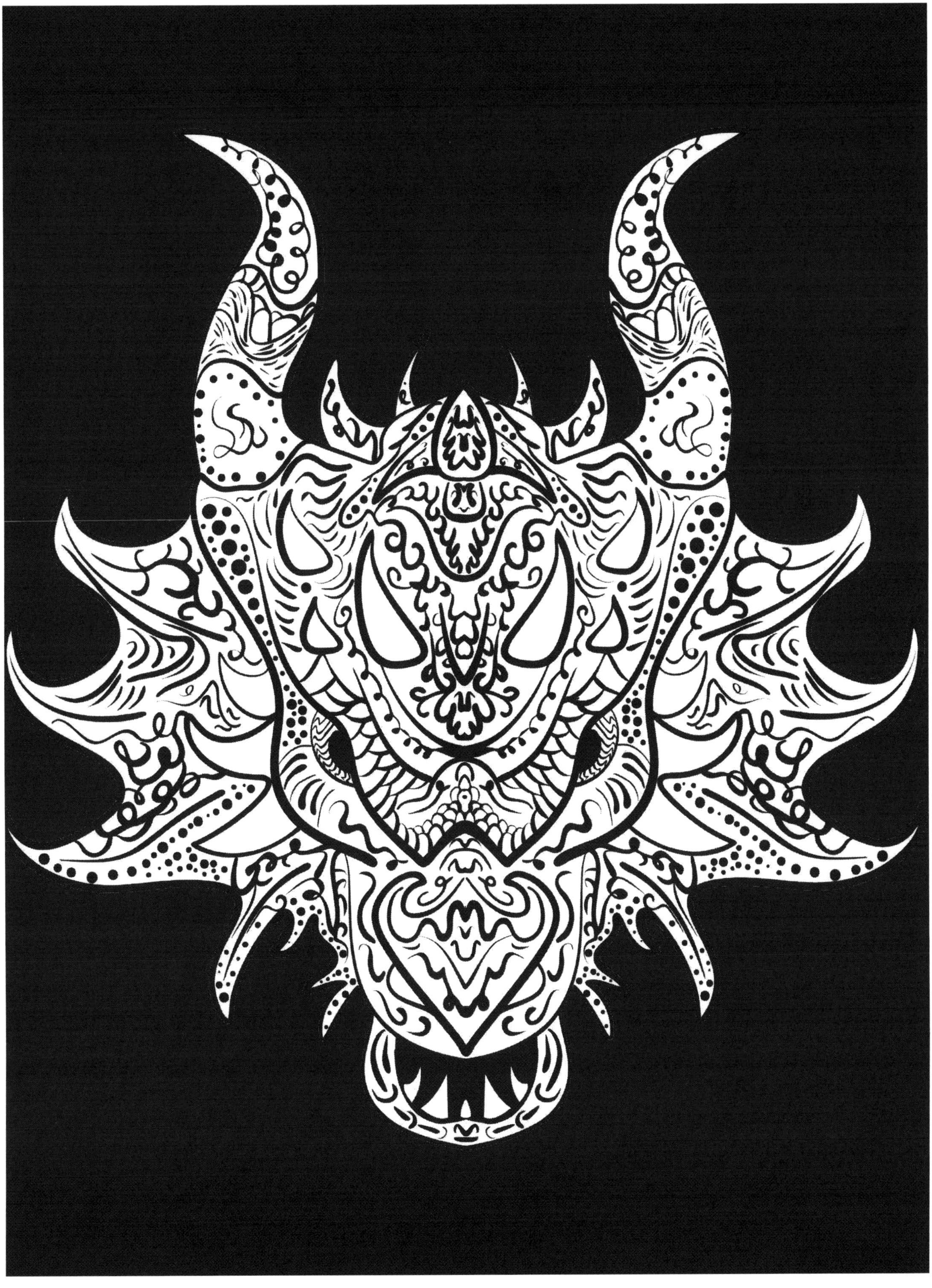

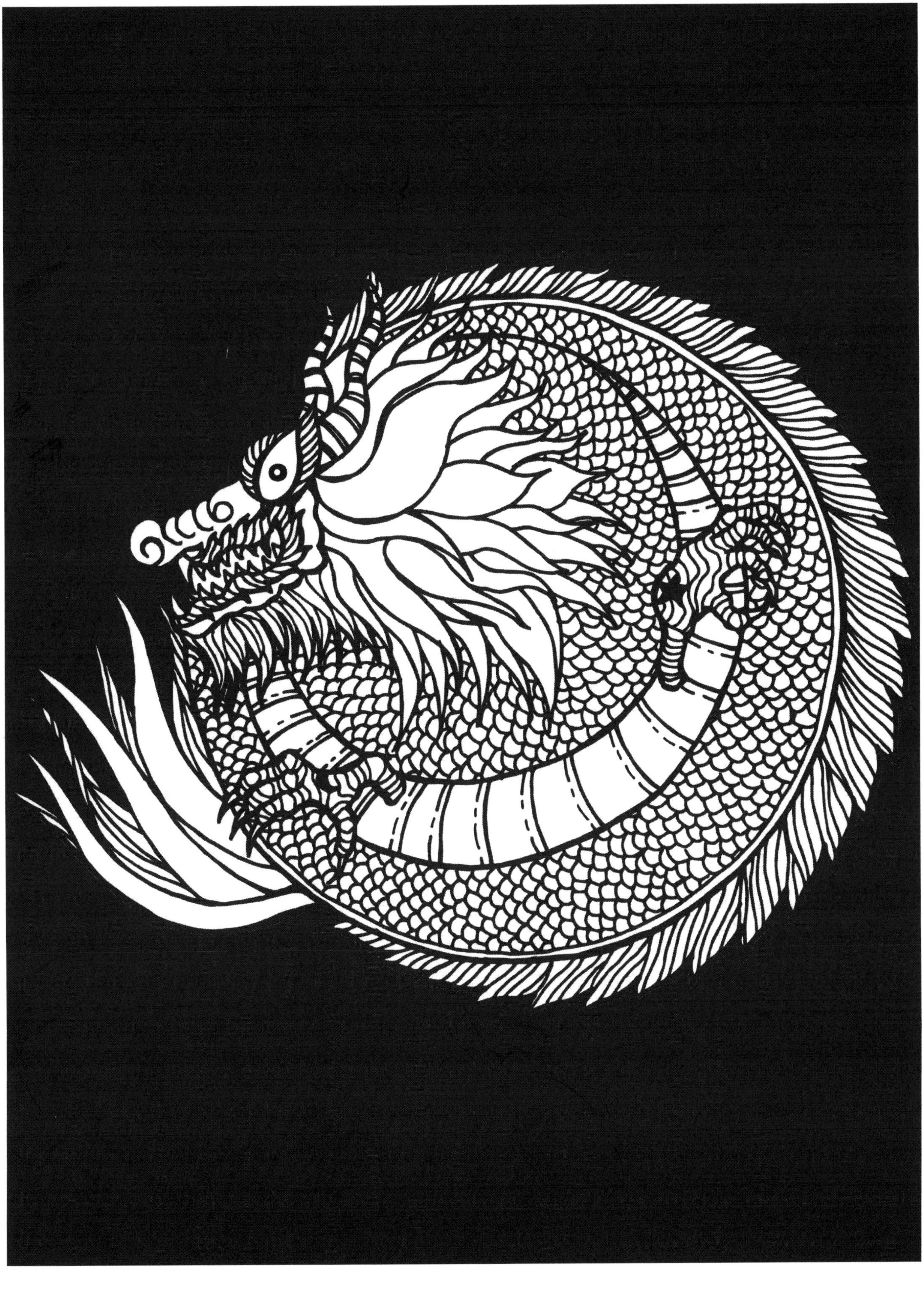

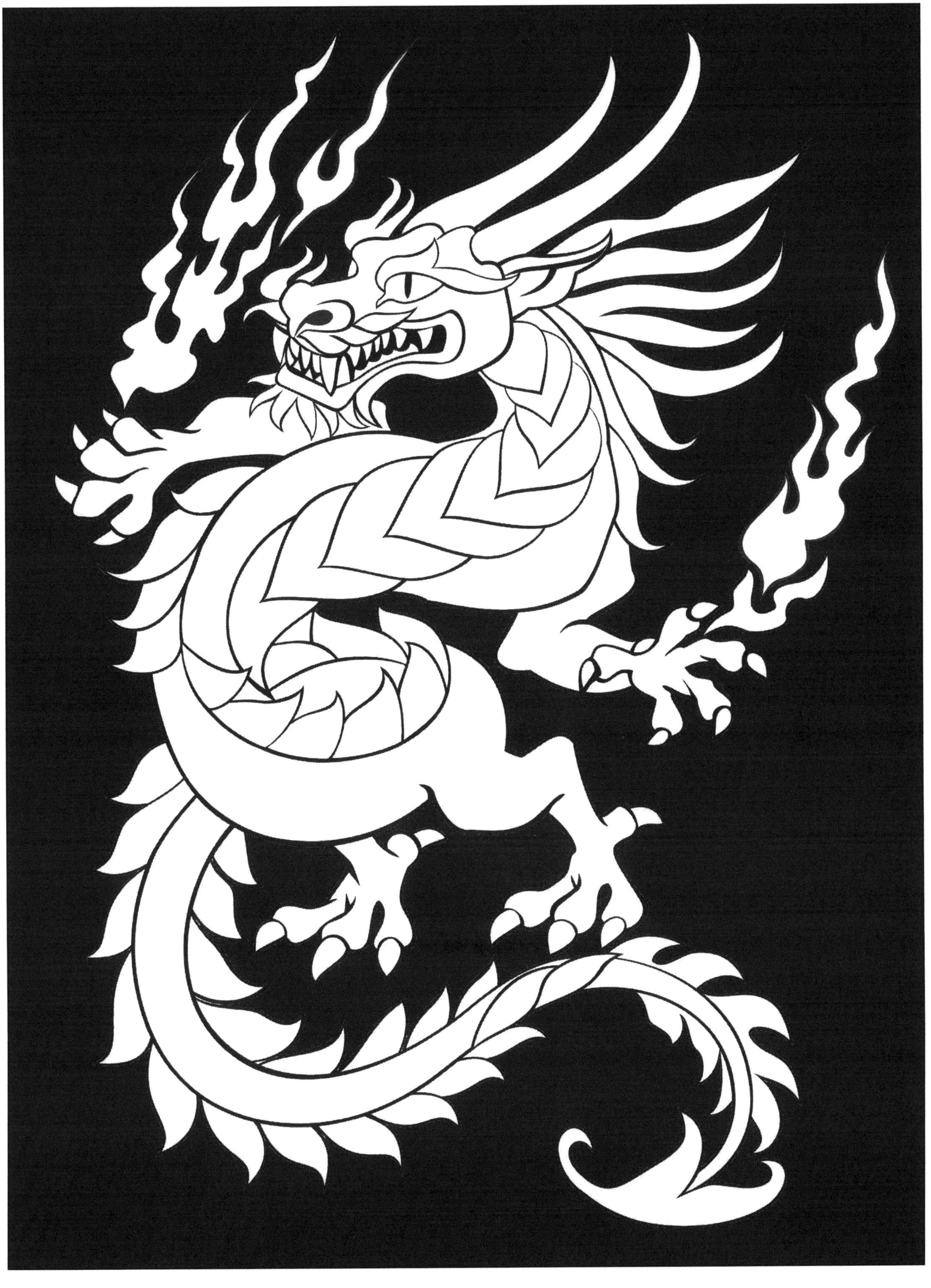

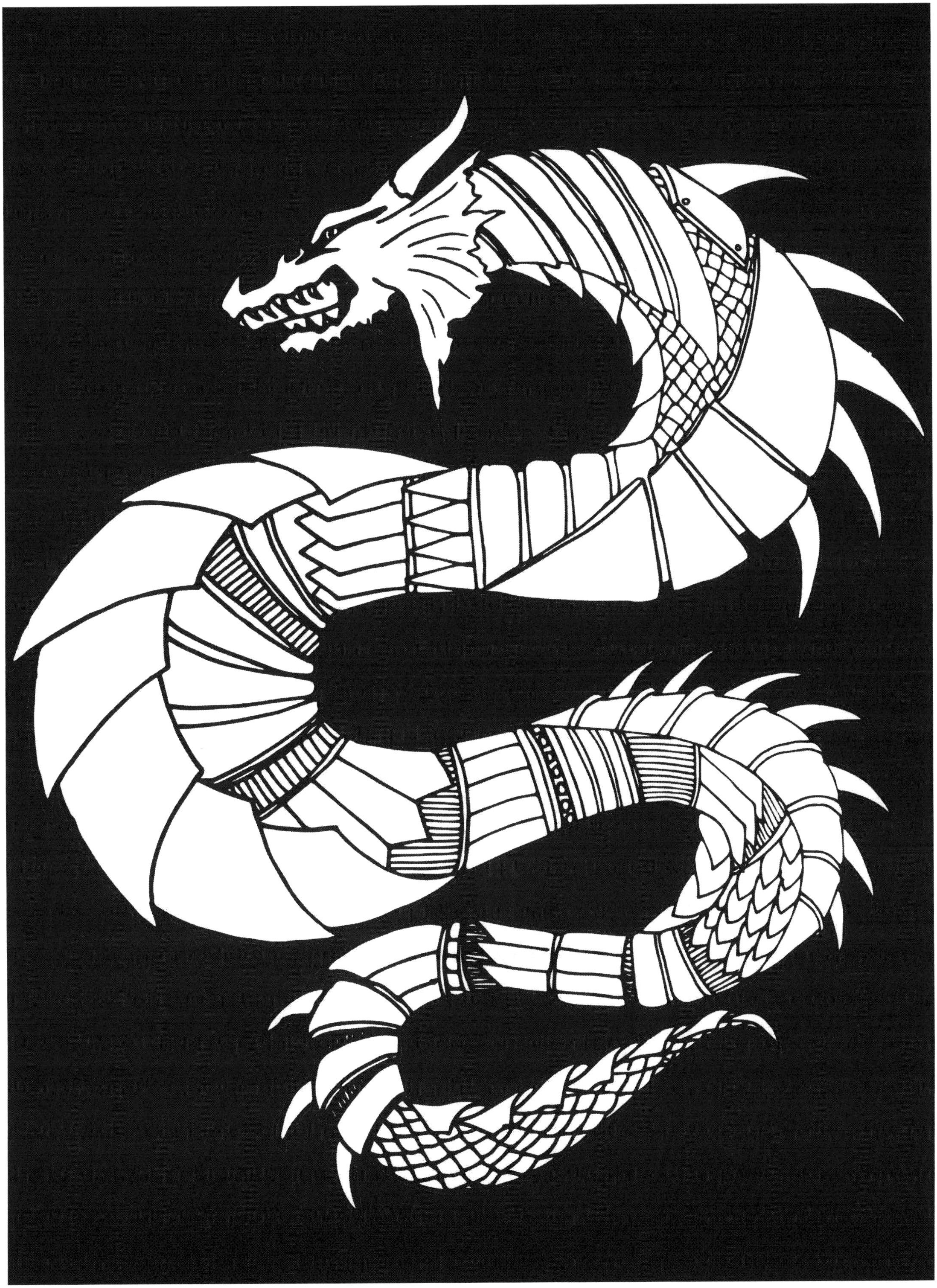

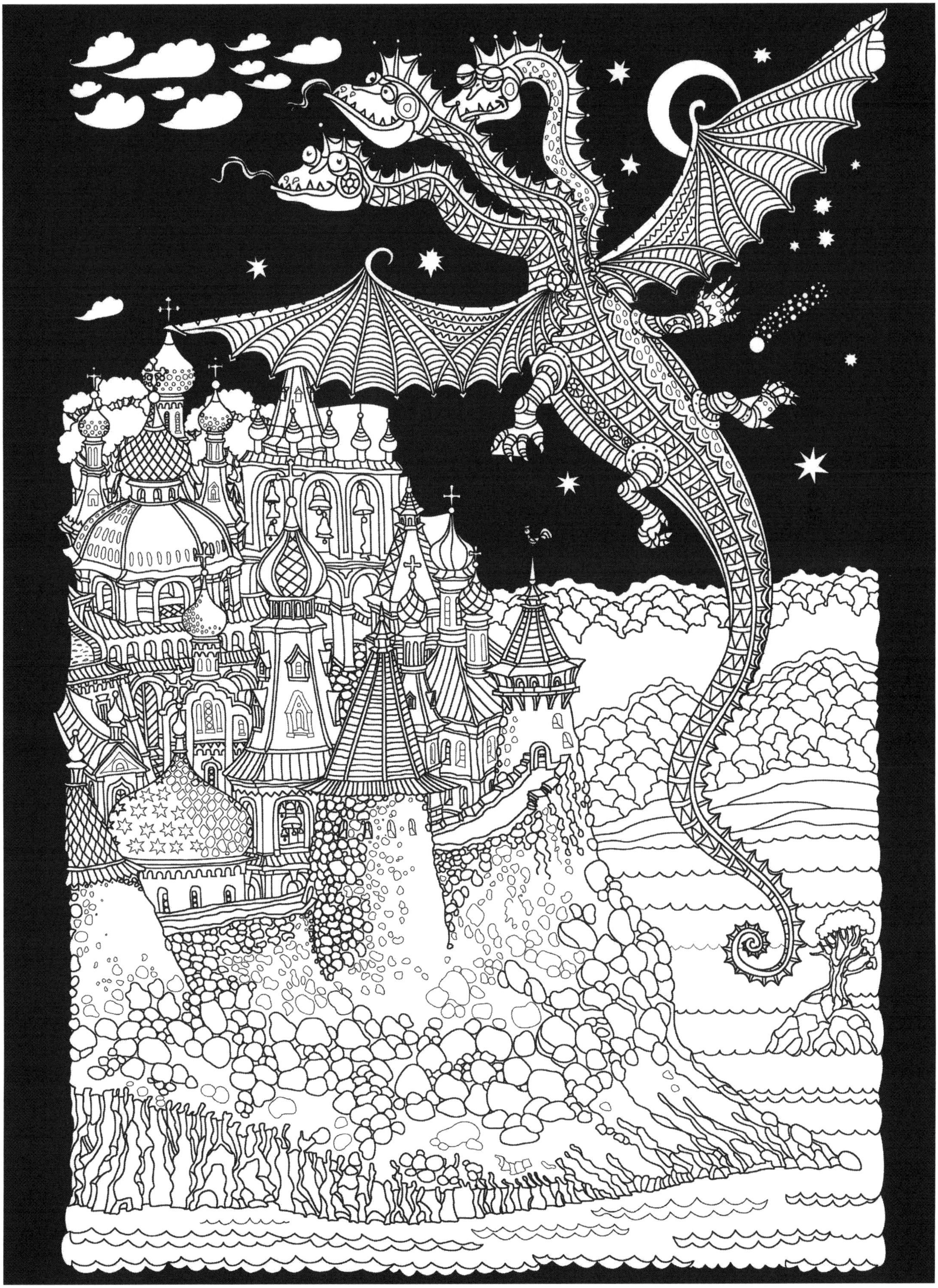

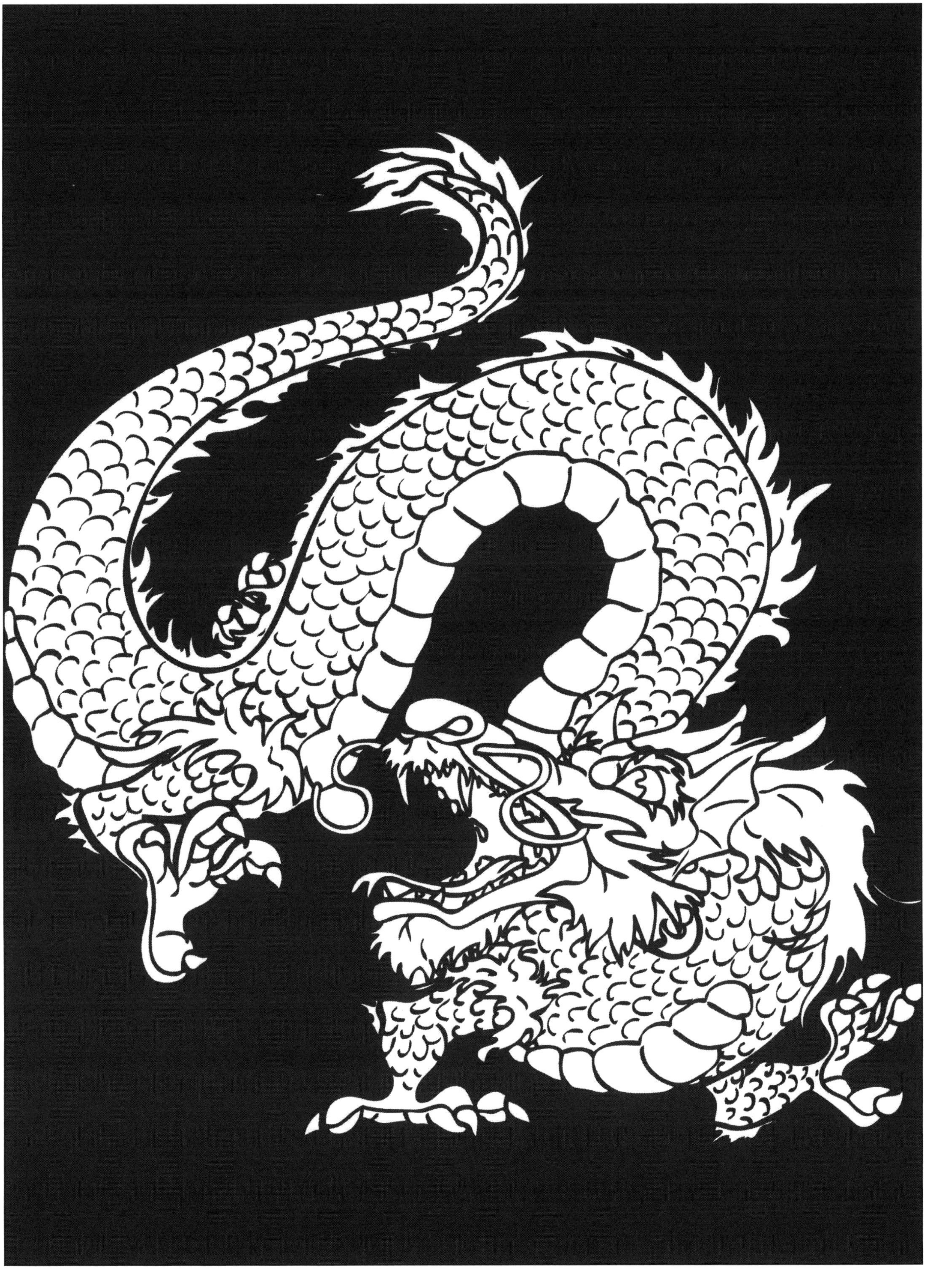

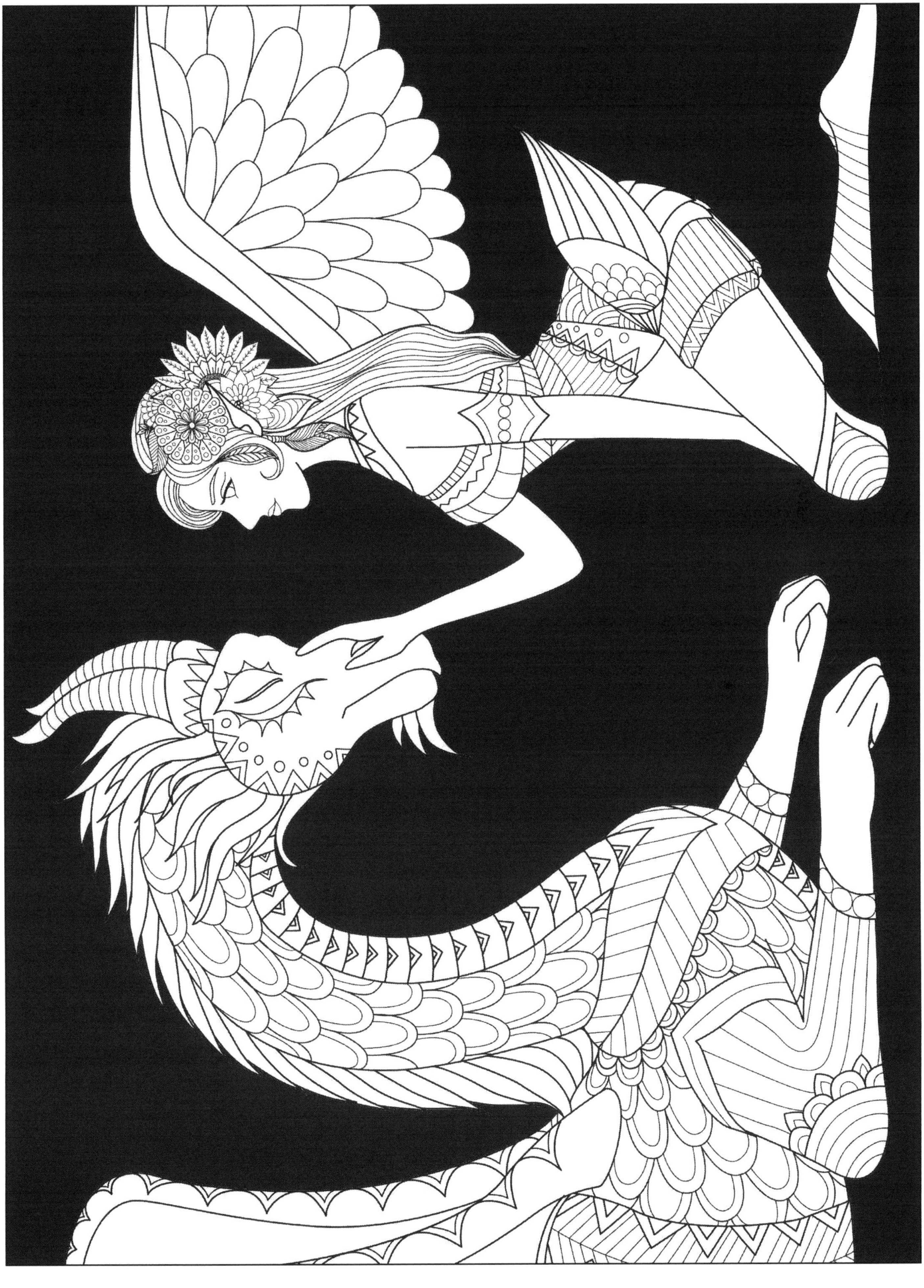

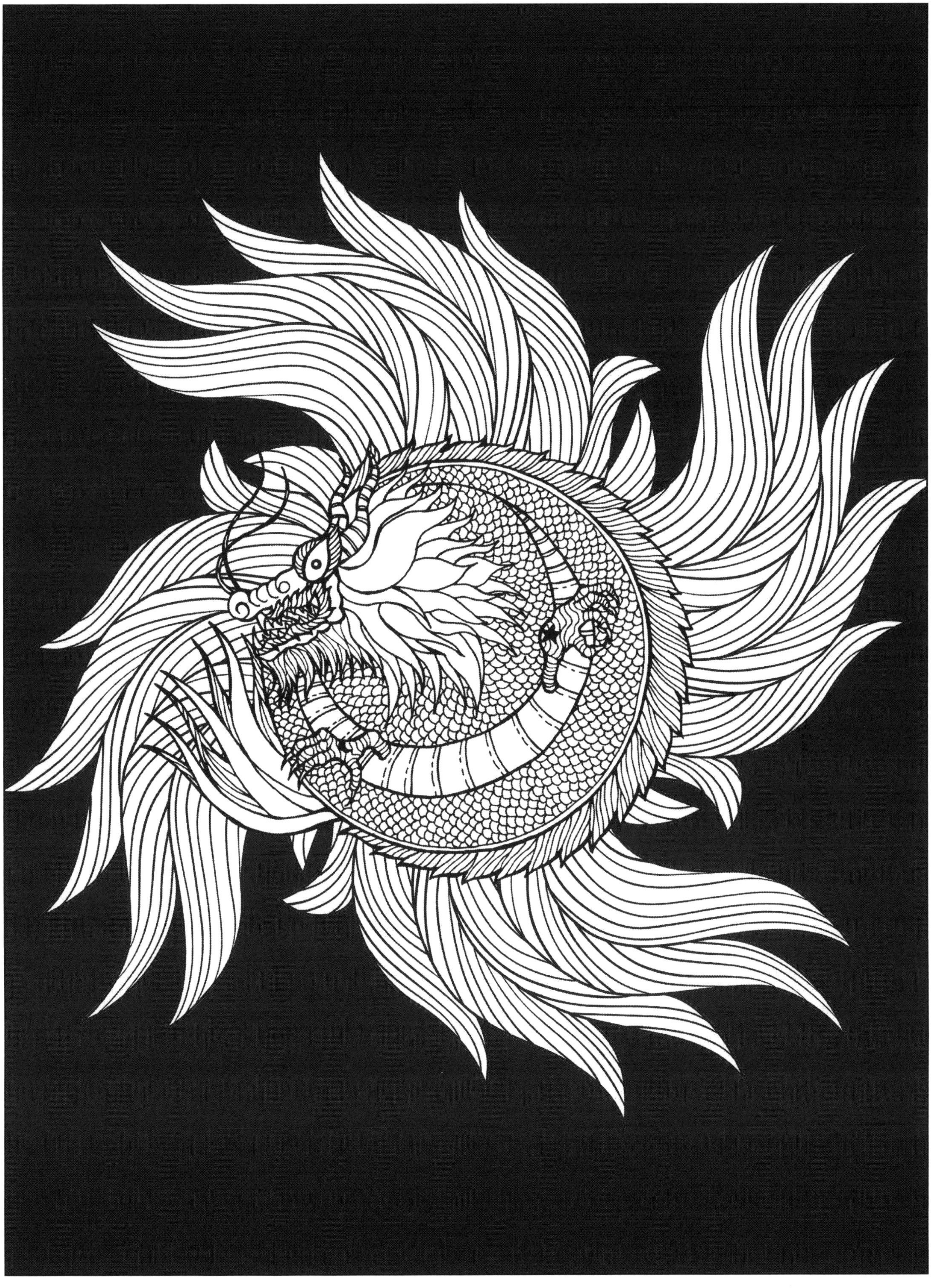

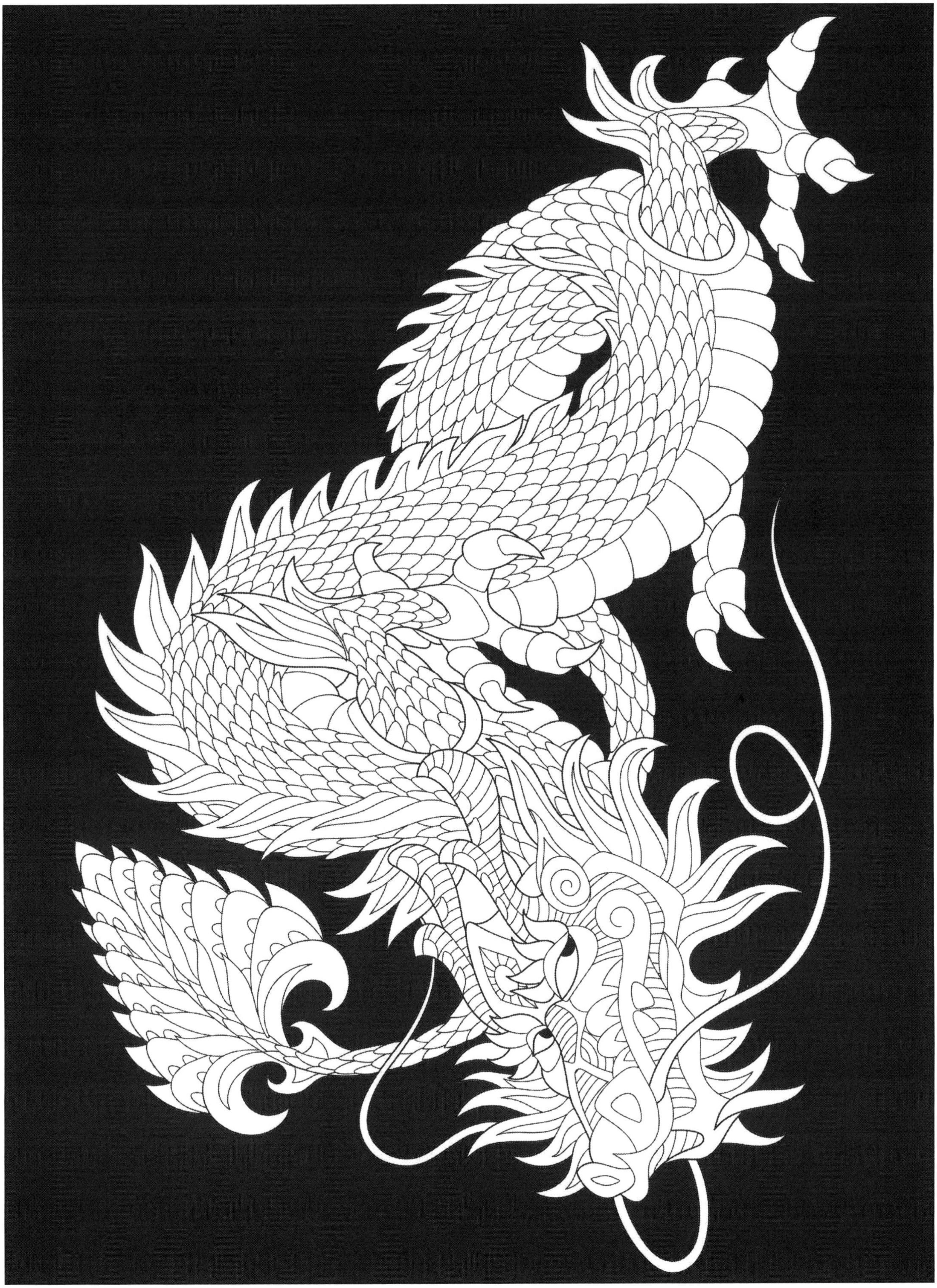

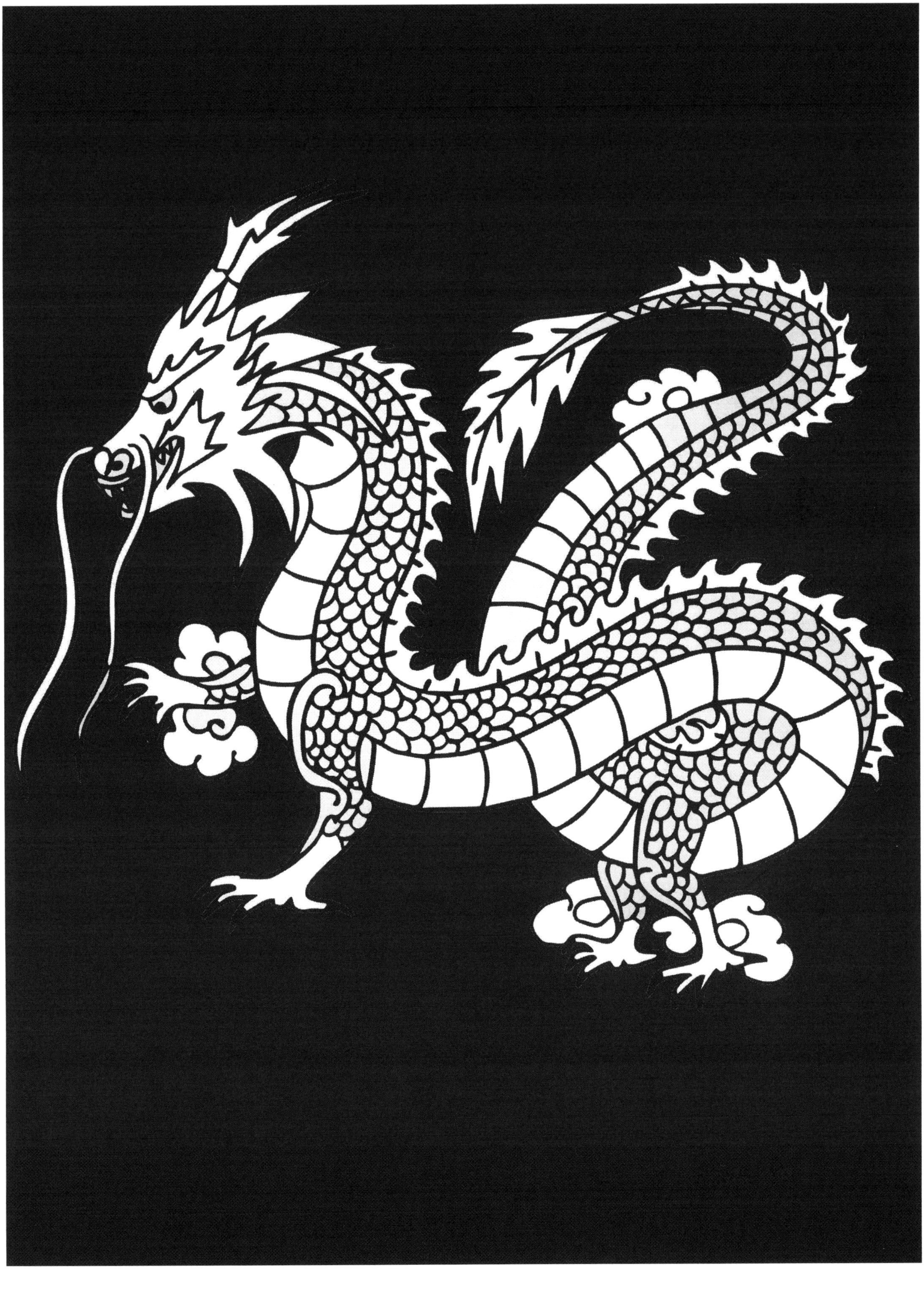

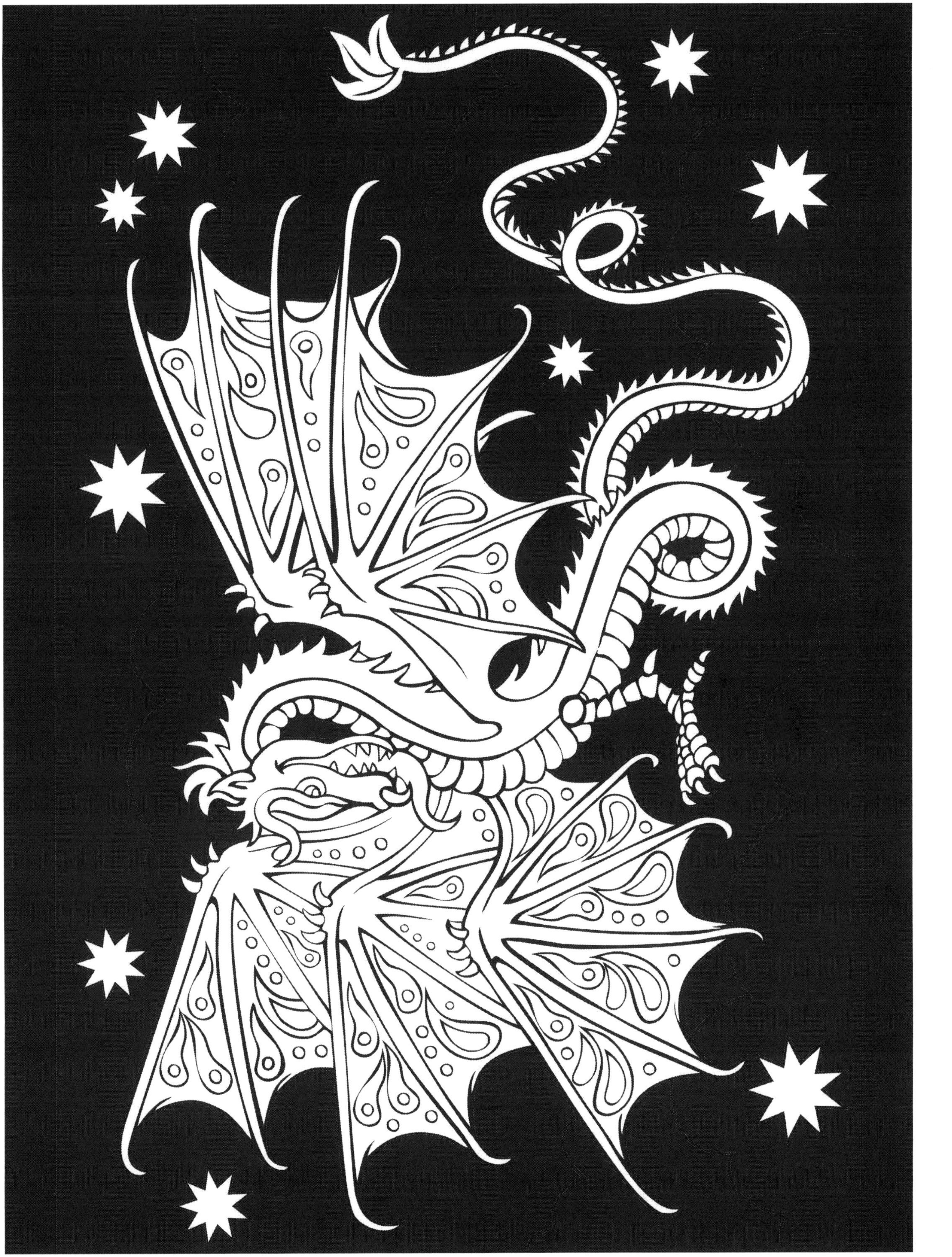

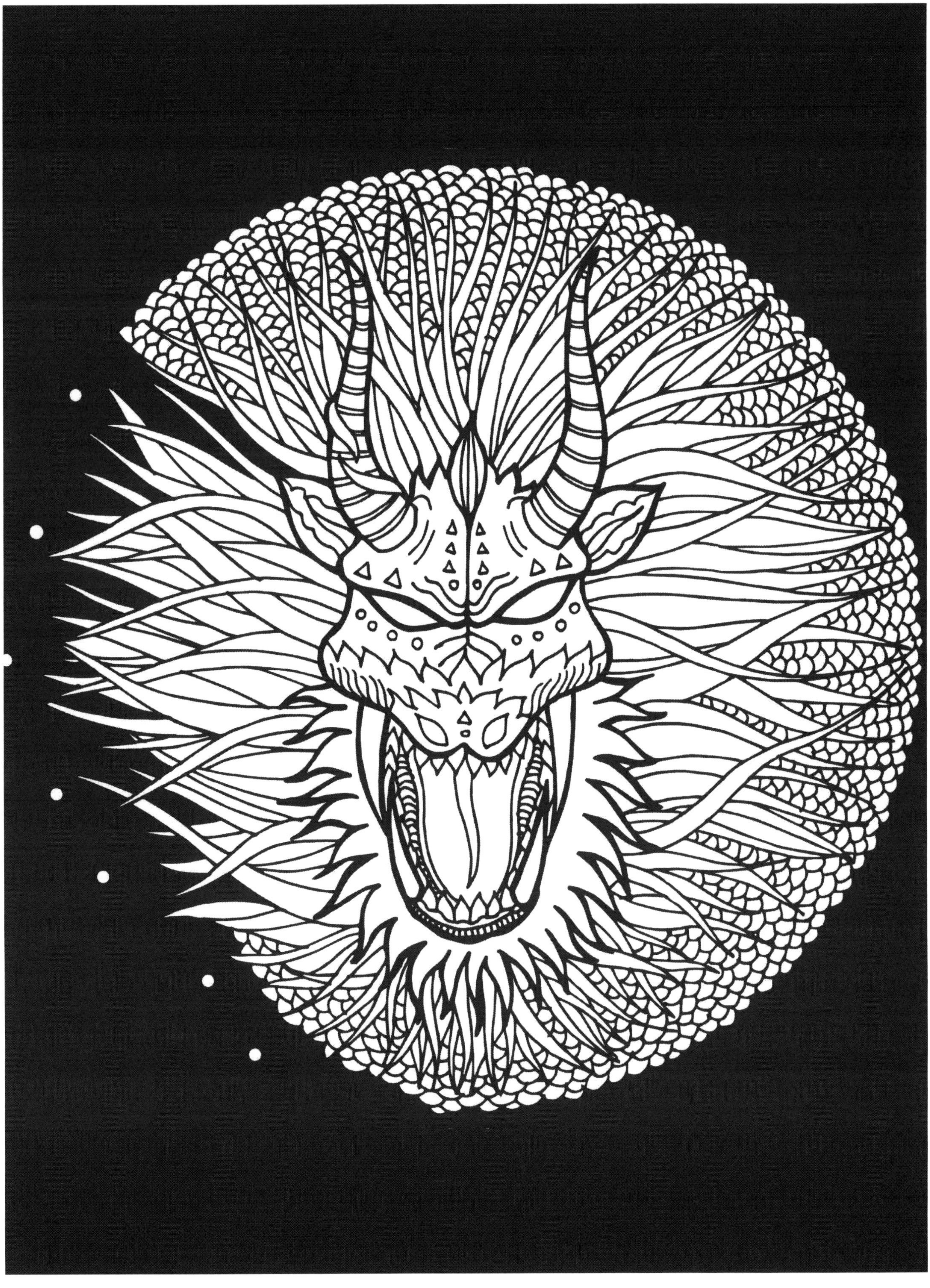

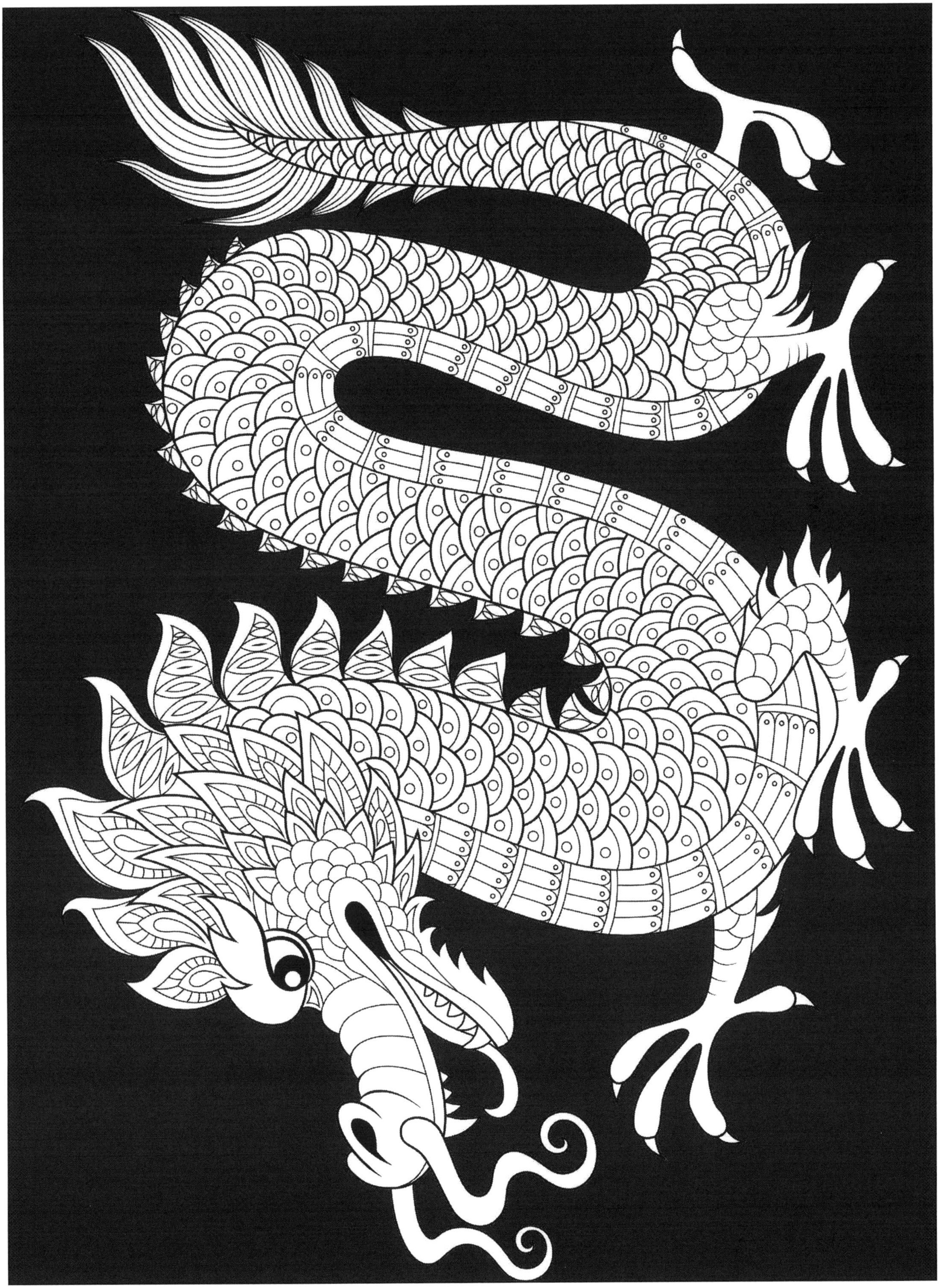

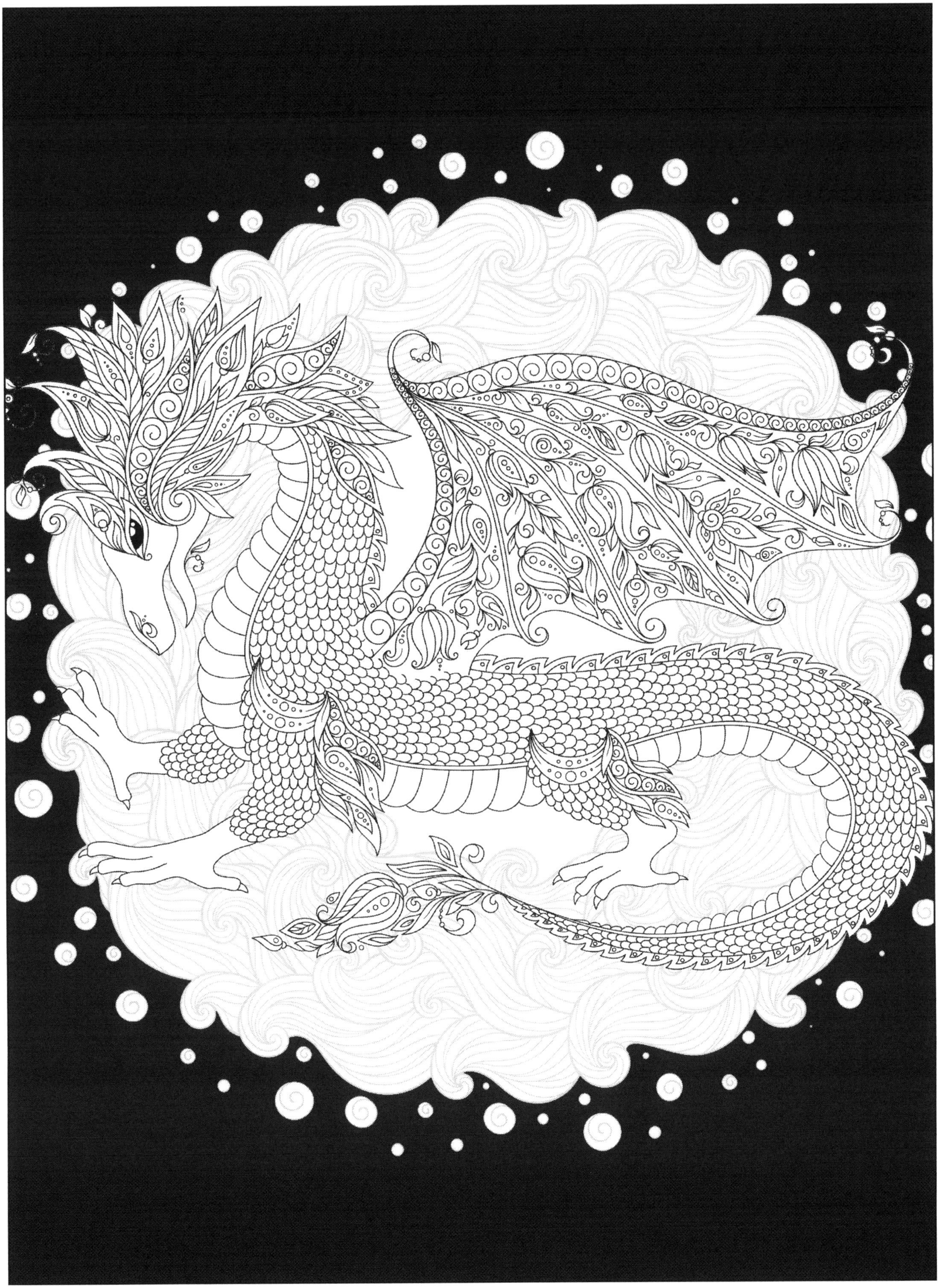

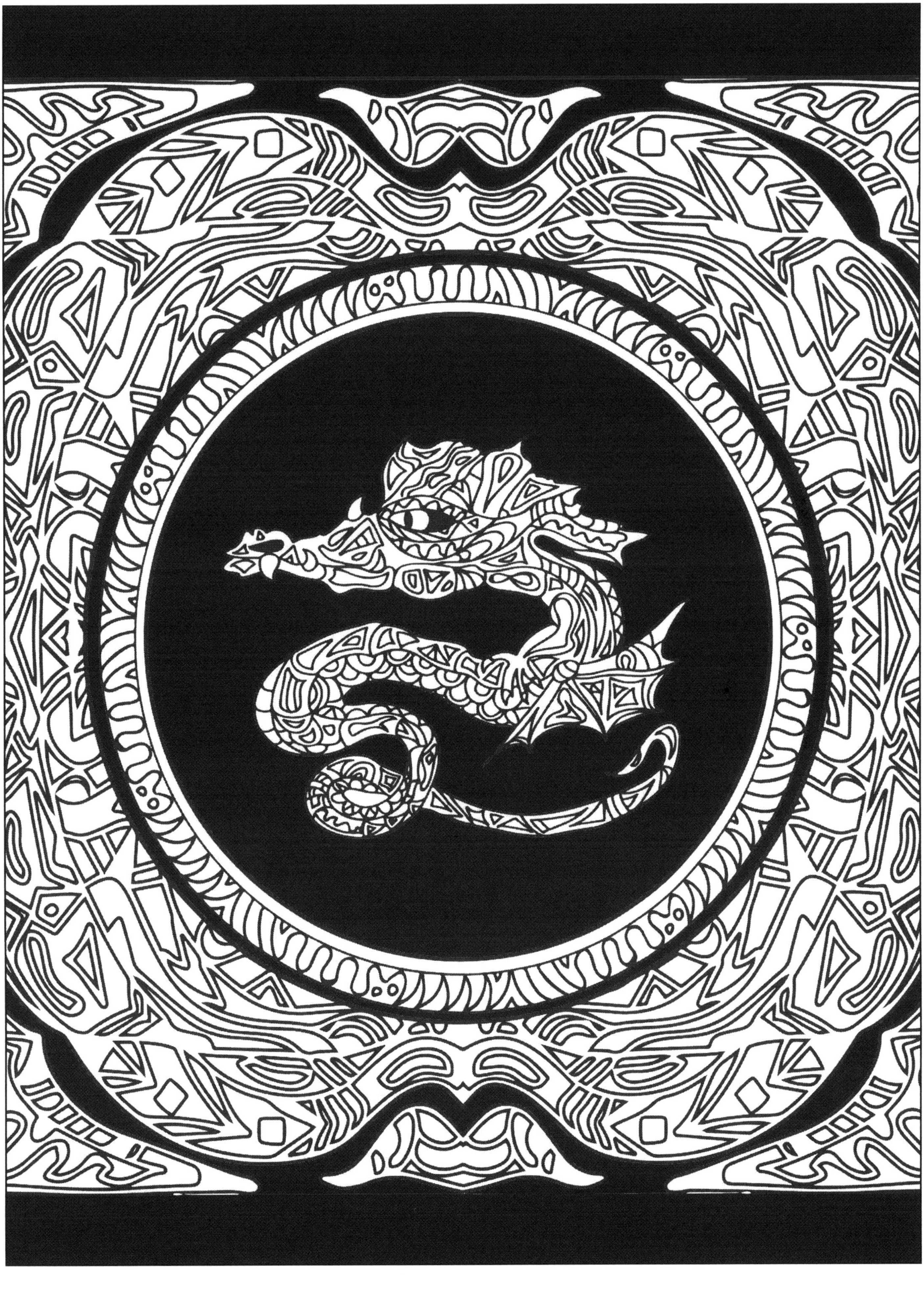

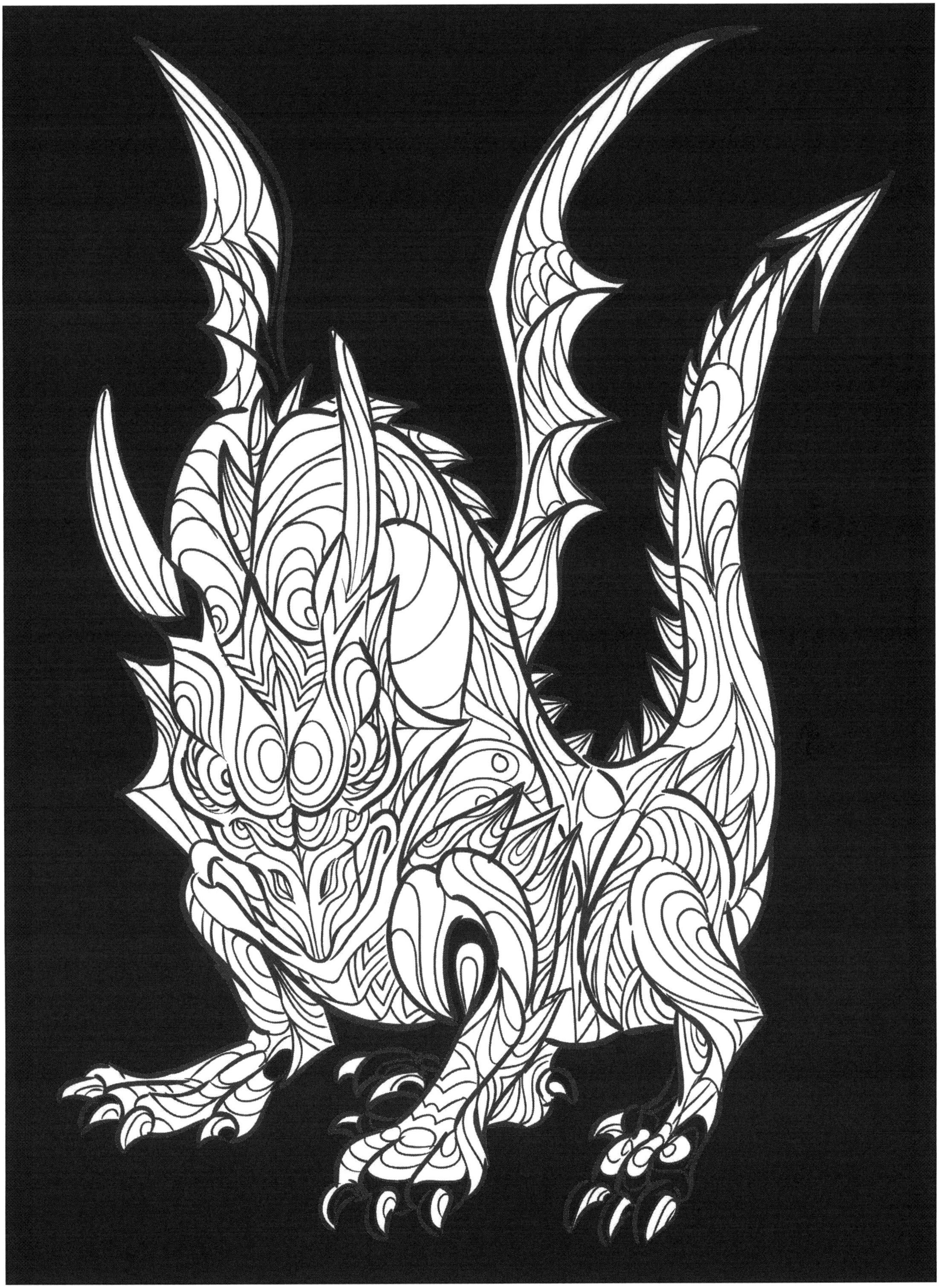

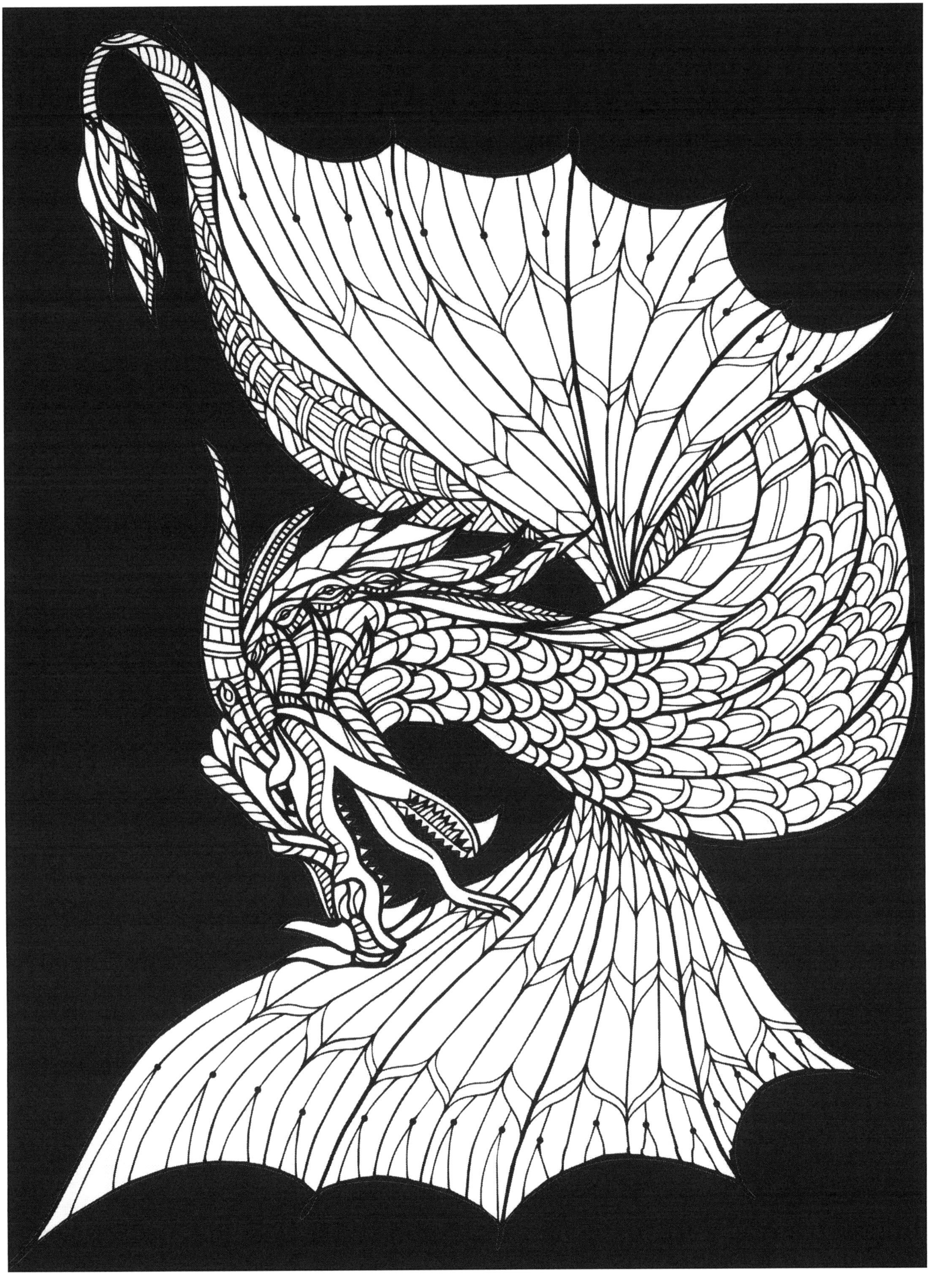

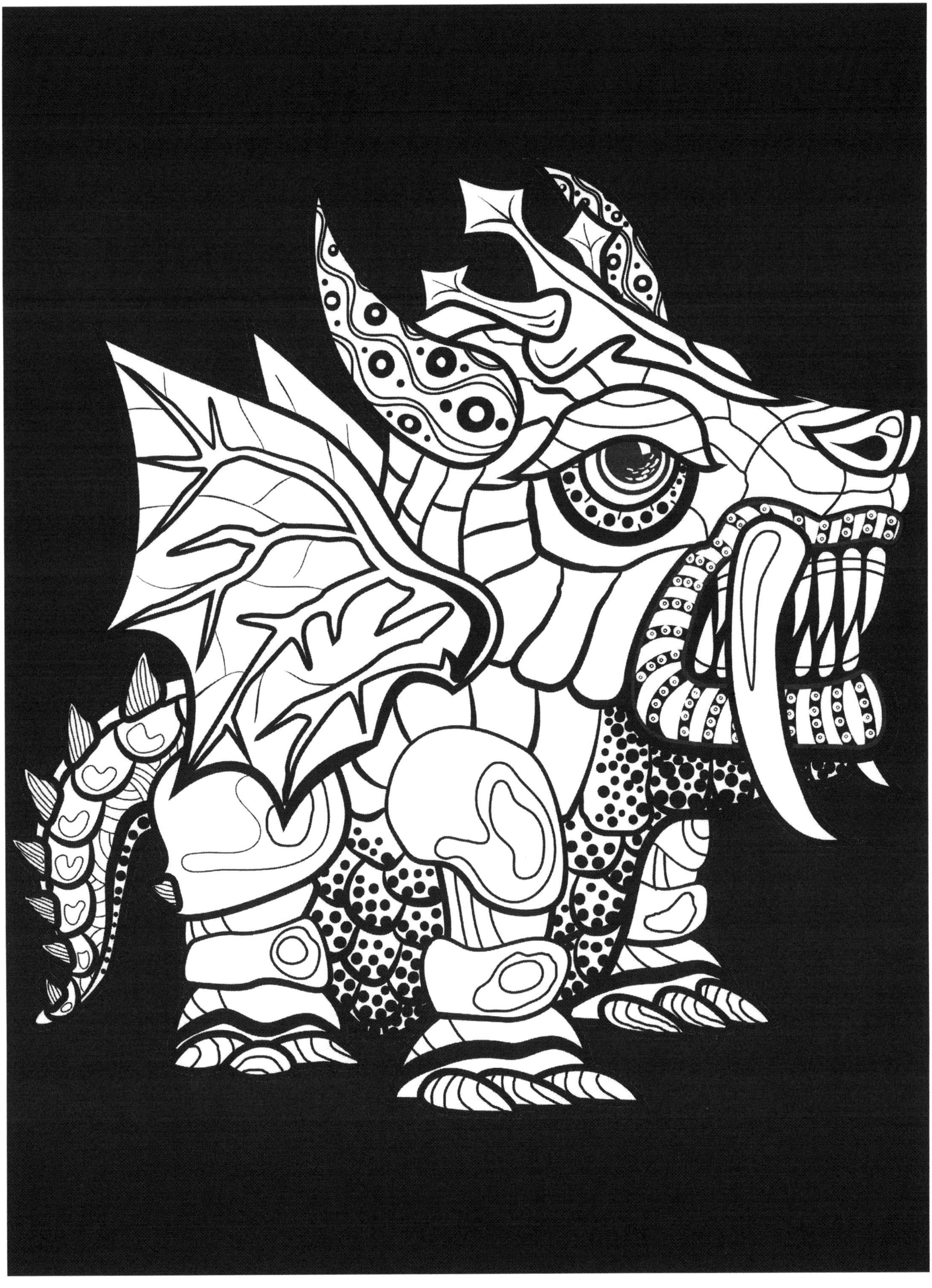

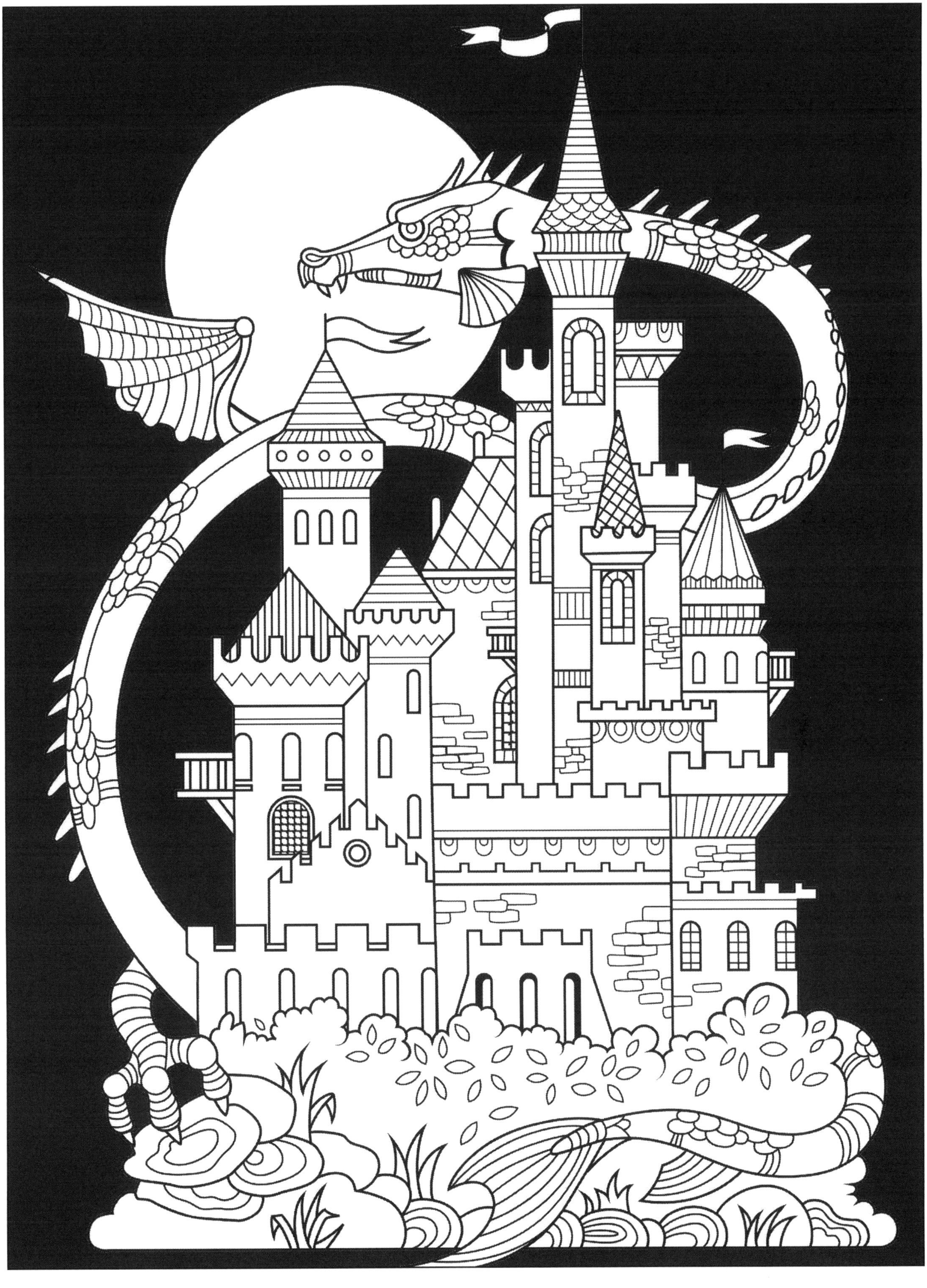

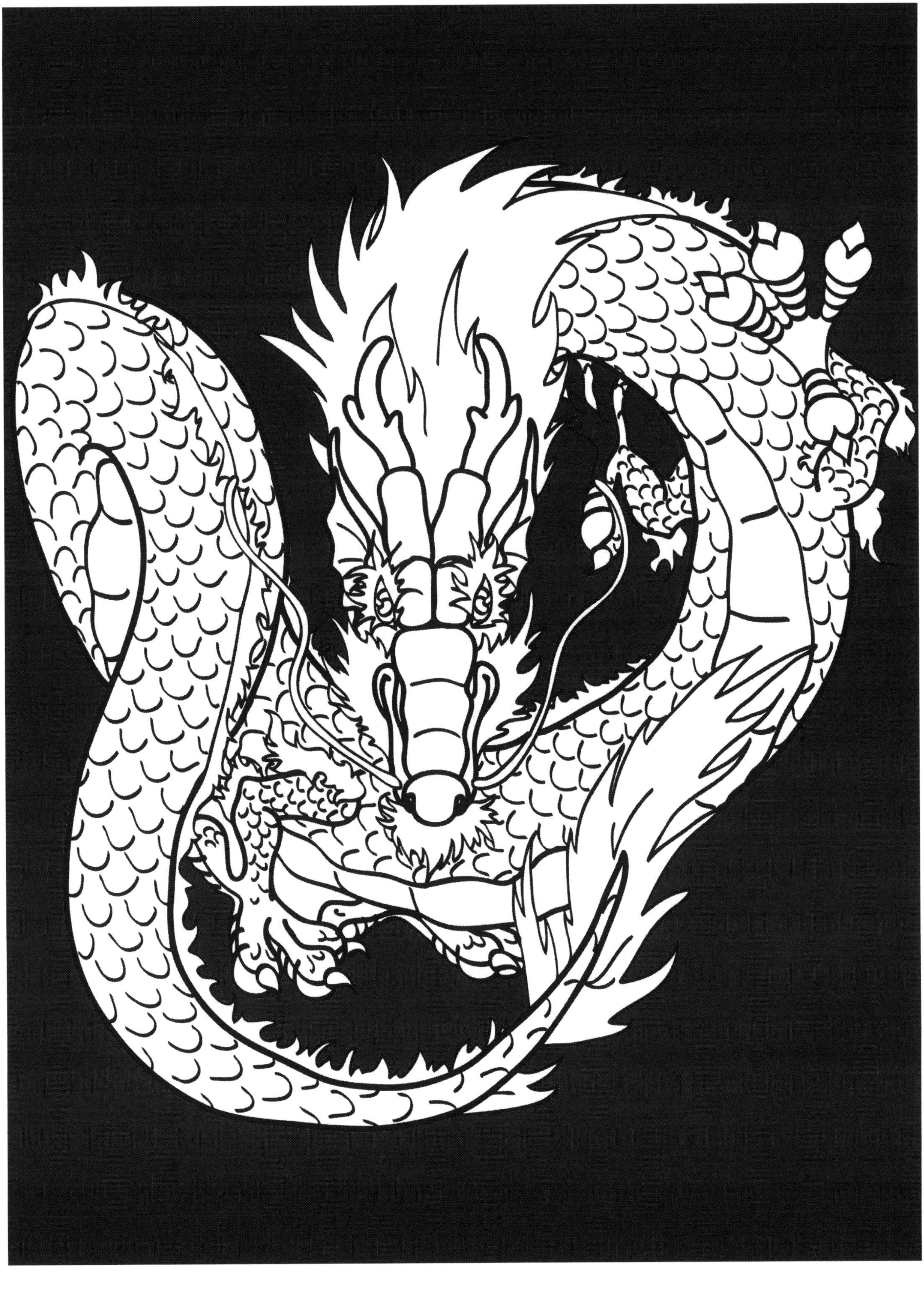

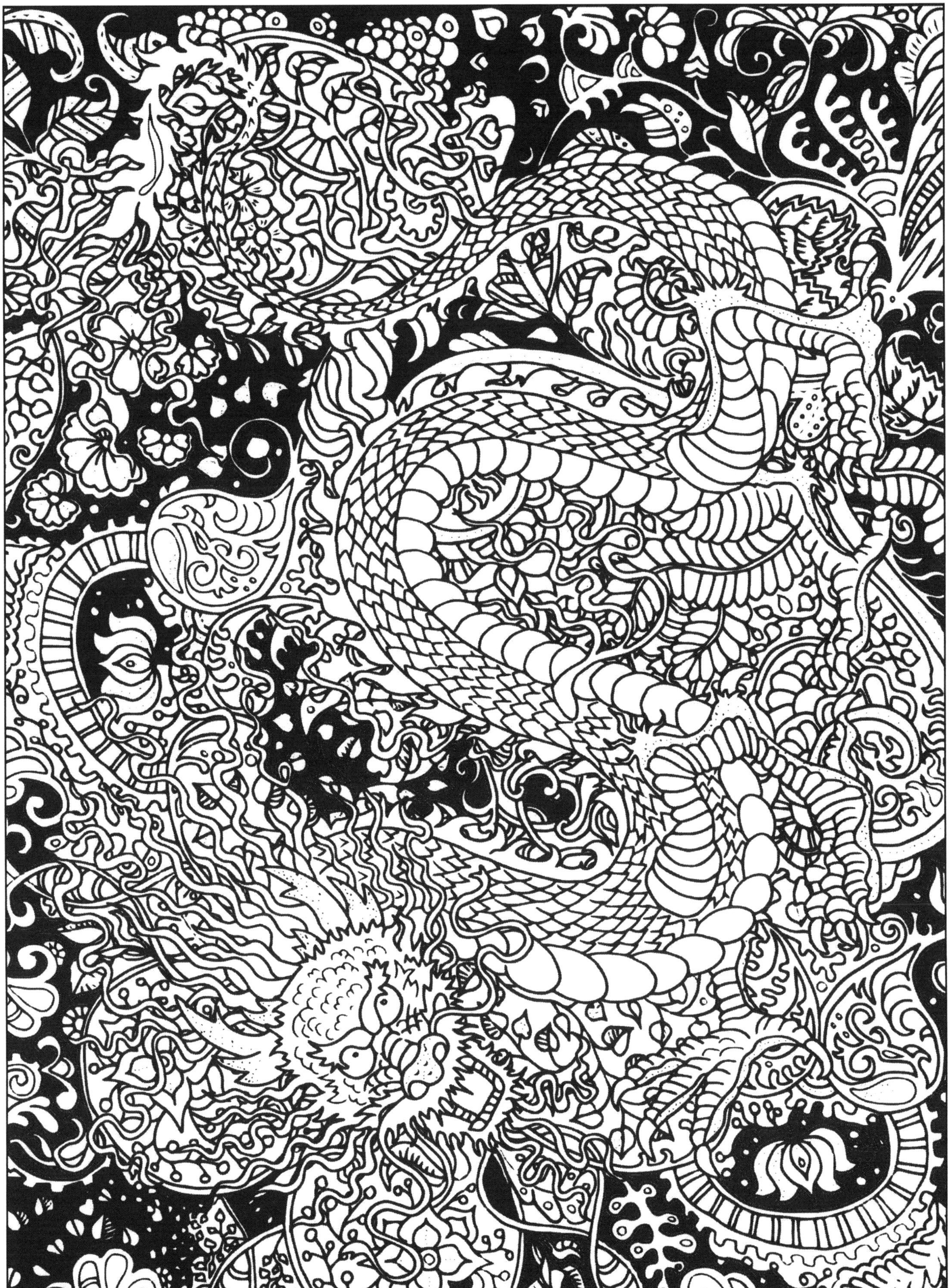